DRAWING
FROM
NATURE

DRAWING
FROM
NATURE

BY JIM ARNOSKY

A Beech Tree Paperback Book 🅱🅱 New York

For Clair and Mary

This new edition is also dedicated to John Burroughs, whose writings deeply affected my outlook on nature, influenced many of the drawing lessons in this book, and continue to inspire my work as an artist.

Library of Congress Cataloging in Publication Data. Arnosky, Jim. Drawing from nature. Summary: Instruction for drawing water, land, plants, and animals. 1.Landscape drawing—Technique—Juvenile literature. 2. Nature (Aesthetics)—Juvenile literature. 3. Animal painting and illustration—Technique—Juvenile literature. [1. Landscape drawing—Technique. 2. Nature (Aesthetics). 3. Animal painting and illustration—Technique. 4.Drawing—Technique.] I. Title NC795.A7 743'.83 82-15327 ISBN 0-688-01295-7 AACR2 ISBN 0-688-07075-2 (pbk.) First Beech Tree Edition, 1995. 10 9 8 7 6 5 4 3

Drawing from nature is discovering the upside down scene through a water drop. It is noticing how much of a fox is tail. Drawing from nature is learning how a tree grows and a flower blooms. It is sketching in the mountains and breathing air bears breathe.

I invite you to sharpen your pencils, your eyesight, and your sense of wonder. Turn to a fresh leaf in your drawing pad and come outdoors.

Jim Arnosky
Ramtails 1982

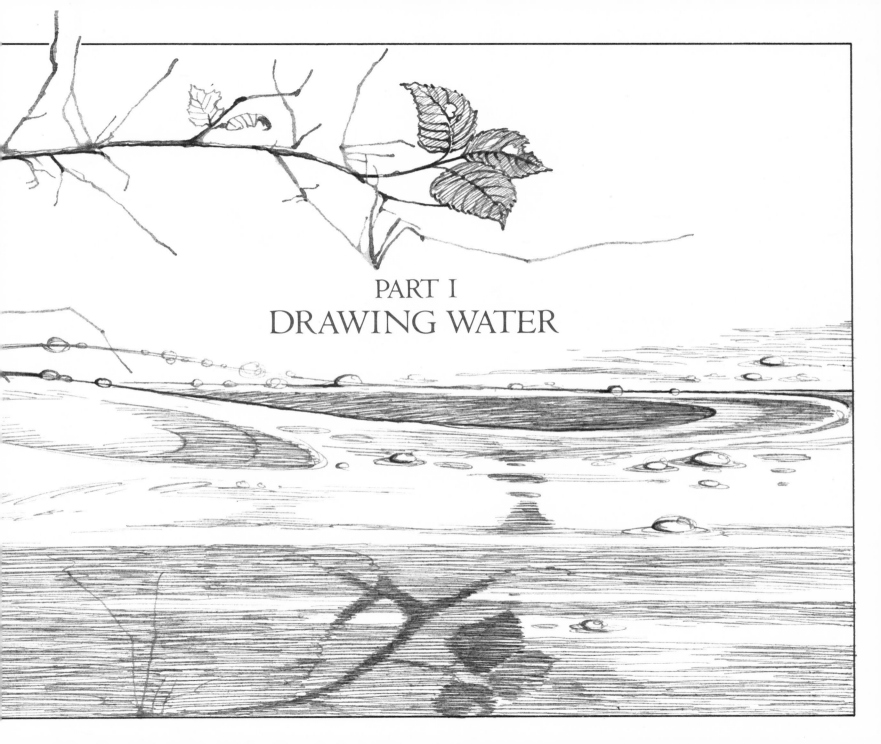

PART I
DRAWING WATER

I can't resist water. It refreshes my senses. It greets my curiosity with a glistening invitation to explore.

Water covers three quarters of the earth's surface. It shapes the land and changes the weather. Water can be liquid, as rainfall; solid, as ice or snow; and gaseous, as fog or steam. The main ingredient in every living organism is water.

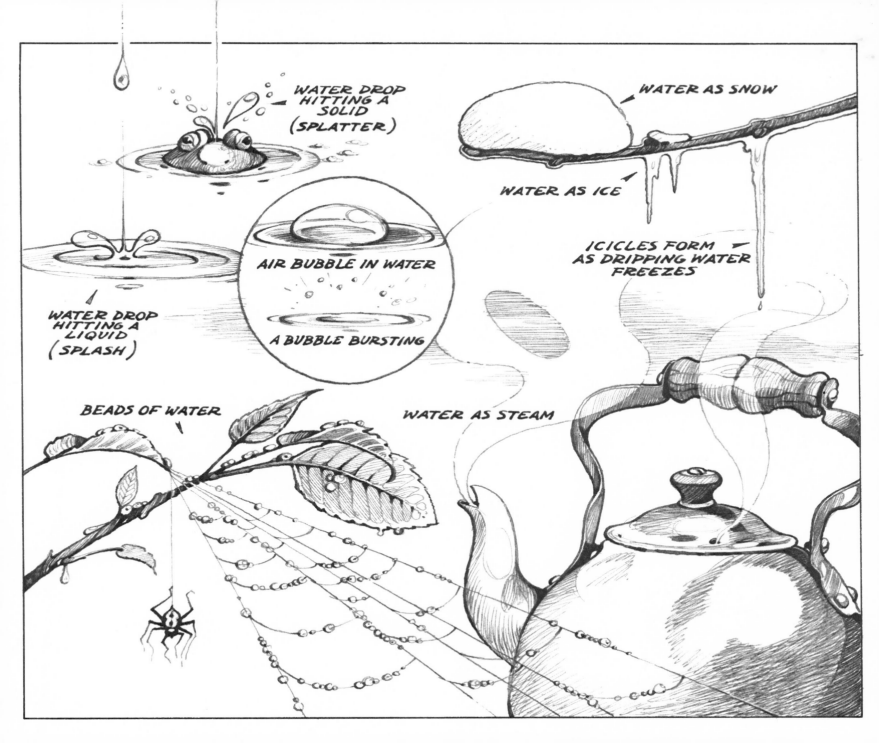

DRAW CLEAR WATER BY SHOWING BOTH THE SURFACE AND THE UNDERWATER DETAIL

DETAIL THE SURFACE ONLY FOR DARK OR MUDDY WATER

Water can dissolve, and mix with, almost every substance. This is why the color of water in nature can be as varied as the places where it is found.

The water in a mountain brook is crystalline, like the sparkling pebbles in its stream bed. Water in a cedar swamp is tea-colored from mixing with the tannic acid in submerged cedar tree stumps.

OFTEN WATER
IN SNOWY COUNTRY
APPEARS INK BLACK

I have seen woodland ponds that were soupy green with algae. Water can also appear to be sky blue, coffee brown, brick red, and ink black.

When you are drawing water from nature, see how it is affected by its surroundings. Add this to your drawings and you will bring home a sense of place in your pictures.

Consider how the water you are drawing relates to the other subjects in your picture. To a water strider skating on a pond, the water is filmlike. It holds the bug up. A swimming frog pushes through water. A sitting duck floats on water. A hovering fish is suspended in water.

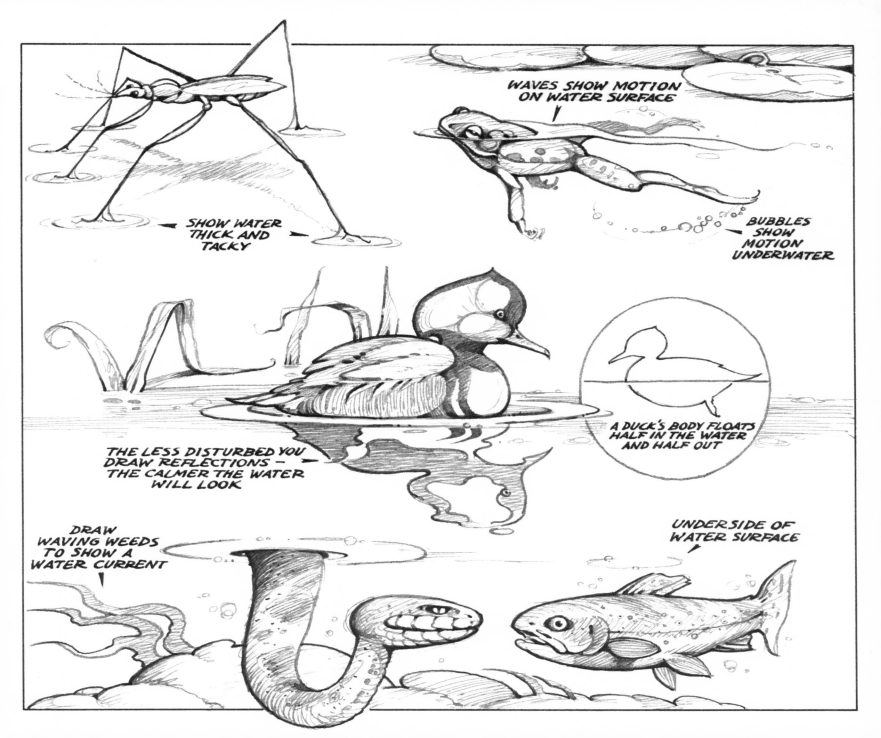

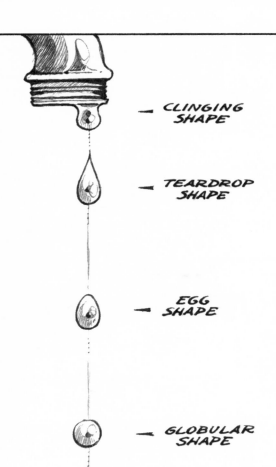

— CLINGING
SHAPE

— TEARDROP
SHAPE

— EGG
SHAPE

— GLOBULAR
SHAPE

— FLATTENED
SPLASH

THE SHAPES OF A WATER DROP
AS IT FALLS THROUGH
THE AIR

Water dripping relentlessly into a sink will wear away the area where the drops land. The slightest flow of water will eventually dig a groove in the surface it runs over. The greater the flow, the wider and deeper the groove. The most majestic river is basically water flowing within the boundaries of its own worn groove.

A stream, large or small, is alive in the movement of its water. Streams are influenced by every feature of the land around them, and, in turn, influence every inch of land they flow over. Streams design their own shores, sculpt their own boulders, and dig their own pools.

When you draw any body of water, draw the effect of the water and the land on each other. By learning where the land shapes the water and where the water shapes the land, you will be able to create a drip, a spill, a flow, and a pool. Your drawings of lakes, streams, rivers, and oceans will look real.

HERE THE LAND SHAPES THE WATER

TAIL OF POOL

SMALL POOLS FORM ON THE DOWNSTREAM SIDES OF OBSTACLES

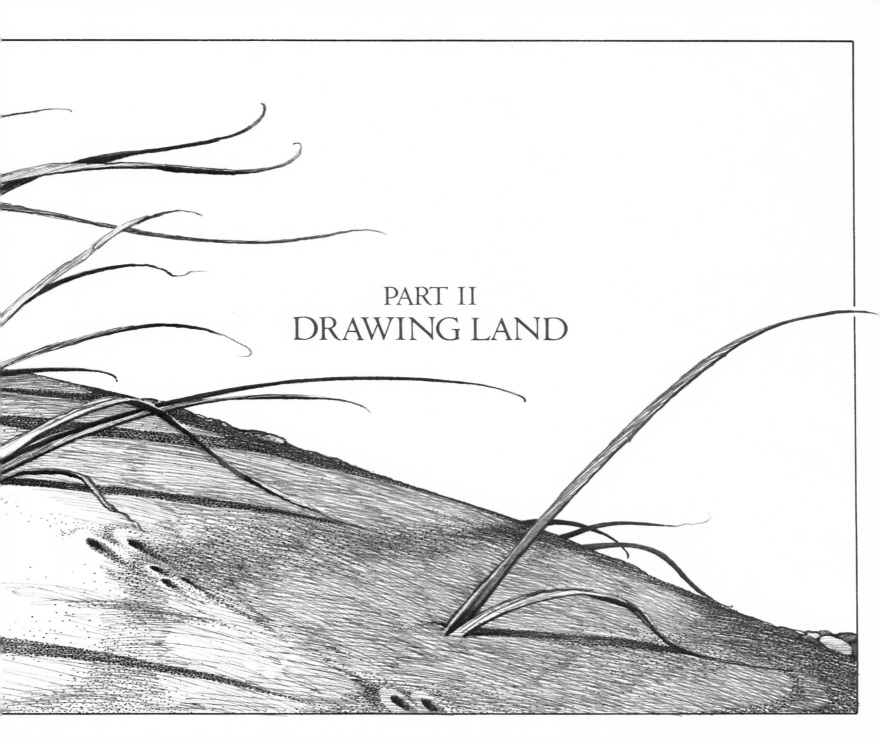

PART II
DRAWING LAND

Climbing over hard rock, walking on spongy marshland—there are times when I am aware of every step I take. I remember a place by the lay of land, and how it feels against my feet.

Land is the surface of the earth that isn't covered by water. It is shaped and changed by inner and outer forces. Some changes happen suddenly. A violent earthquake or volcanic eruption can alter the land in minutes. Most changes happen slowly. A seashore changes a little every day from the wear of surf and wind.

The ocean grinds rocks into sand and molds sand into beach. The wet beach is the twilight zone between water and land. It is where the ocean deposits broken shells, loosened seaweed, and other drifted debris. Here shorebirds walk, searching for morsels of food. Everything on a wet beach looks as if it has just arrived.

DRAW CRISP HIGHLIGHTS
FOR A WET OR SHINY LOOK

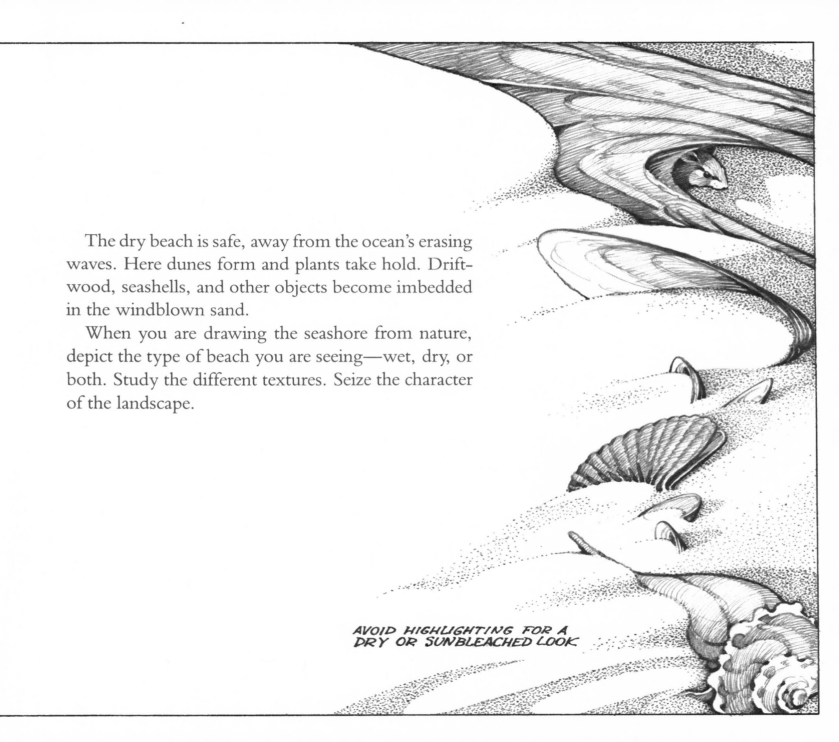

The dry beach is safe, away from the ocean's erasing waves. Here dunes form and plants take hold. Driftwood, seashells, and other objects become imbedded in the windblown sand.

When you are drawing the seashore from nature, depict the type of beach you are seeing—wet, dry, or both. Study the different textures. Seize the character of the landscape.

AVOID HIGHLIGHTING FOR A DRY OR SUNBLEACHED LOOK

Add a sense of depth and distance to your pictures by drawing the horizon line first. Then, in a series of steps, lightly sketch the features of land farthest away and work forward, in perspective, to those nearest to you. Once you have outlined the land features, and any structures on them, give your picture dimension by adding shading and detail.

Study the river scene on the opposite page. It was drawn as I have described. Look at the finished drawing and see how it breaks down into the five steps shown.

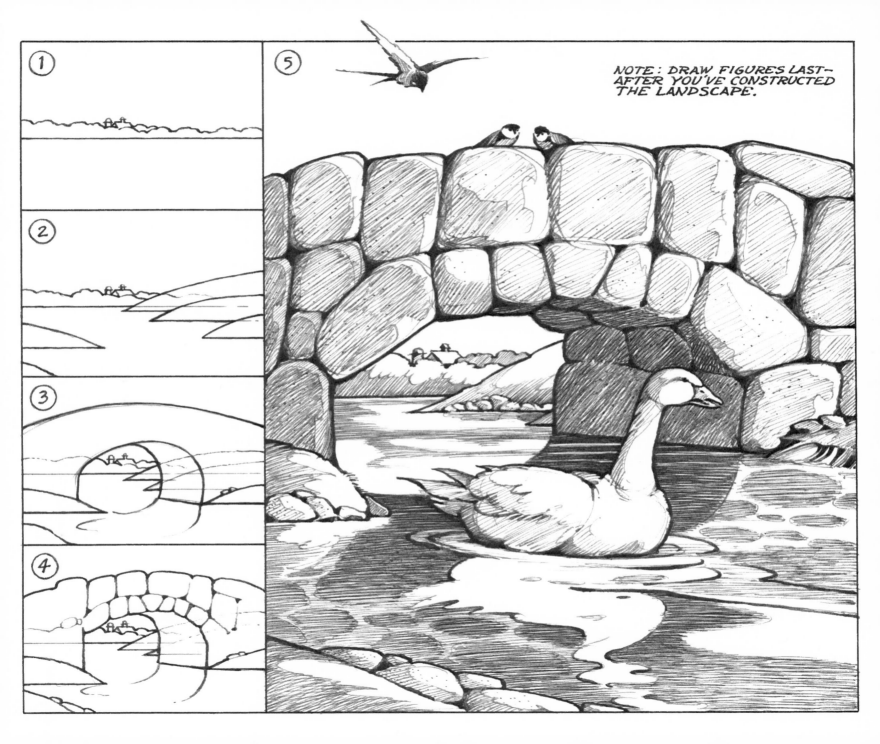

In hill country, walls of stone cleared from the land are common. Originally they divided farms into meadows, pastures, and woodlots. Now they are worn with age and have been reclaimed by nature. If you find one, sketch it as a study in basic construction.

Pile each stone in your drawing as the farmer did, beginning with the largest boulders on the bottom. Then make sure each new layer of stones is placed firmly and will support the next. Your drawing will be as solid as the enduring wall itself.

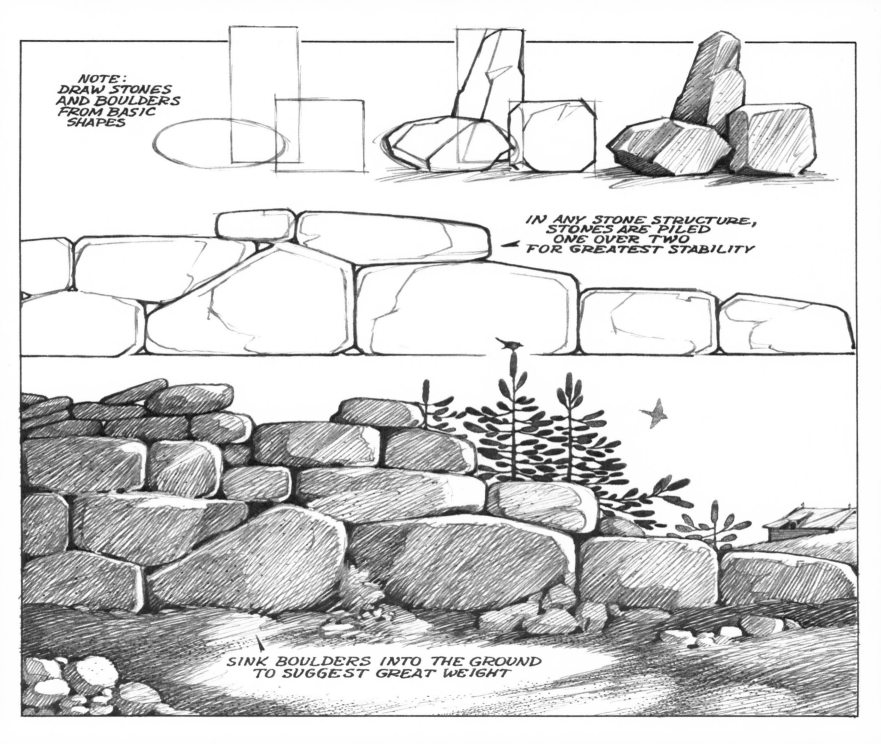

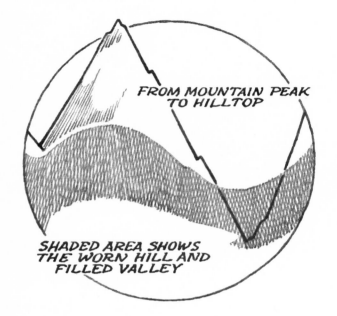

FROM MOUNTAIN PEAK
TO HILLTOP

SHADED AREA SHOWS
THE WORN HILL AND
FILLED VALLEY

Hills and valleys are very old land forms. Erosion wears earth off a hill and washes it down slopes to the valley floor. A little round hill and a gently sloping valley may once have been a towering mountain and a deep ravine.

Drawing hills without trees is a simple matter of shaping with stippling or line shading. Drawing a wooded hill is more difficult. In leaf, it is a study in treetops. Leaf bare, it is a character study of the hill's worn spine.

TO CONSTRUCT A SPARSELY-LEAFED SPRING OR AUTUMN HILLSIDE, DRAW TRUNKS AND BRANCHES IN TREETOPS

TO CONSTRUCT A FULLY-LEAFED SUMMER HILLSIDE, DRAW THE TREETOPS ONLY

LIGHT FROM LEFT

LIGHT HEAD-ON

LIGHT FROM RIGHT

The earth is always working on its mountains—rounding and smoothing old ones, raising new ones. Most mountains are formed by the earth's crust shifting, wrinkling, folding, or swelling. Others are the result of running water or ice, carving into the land.

When you are drawing mountains from nature, try to determine how they may have been formed. Then form them that way with your line strokes.

SHADING IS ESPECIALLY IMPORTANT
WHEN YOU ARE DRAWING MOUNTAINS....
PROPER SHADING DEPENDS ON LIGHT
DIRECTION AND ITS PLAY ON SURFACE SHAPES

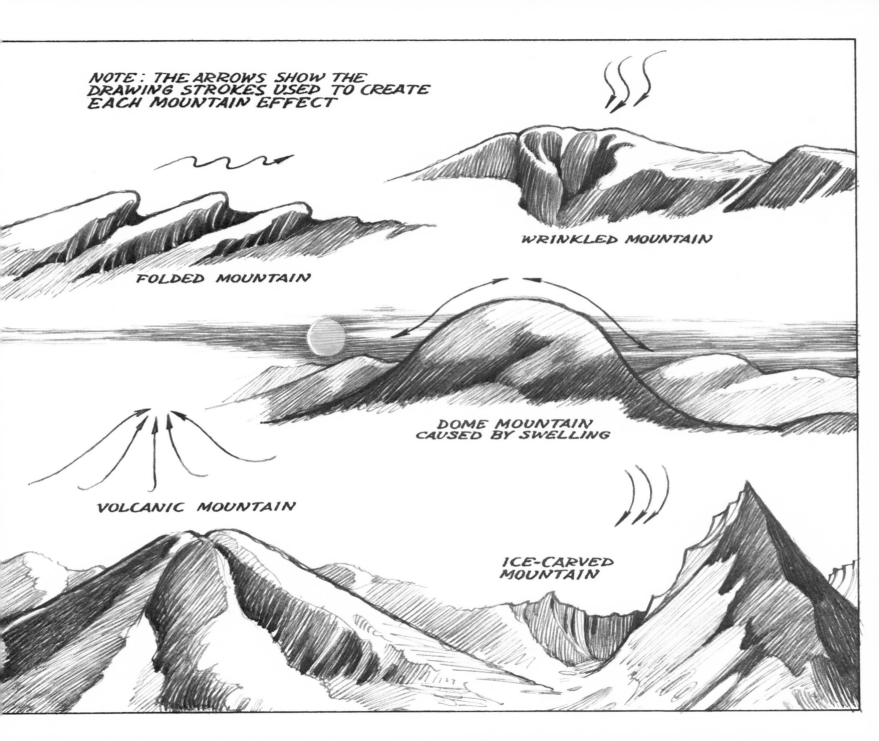

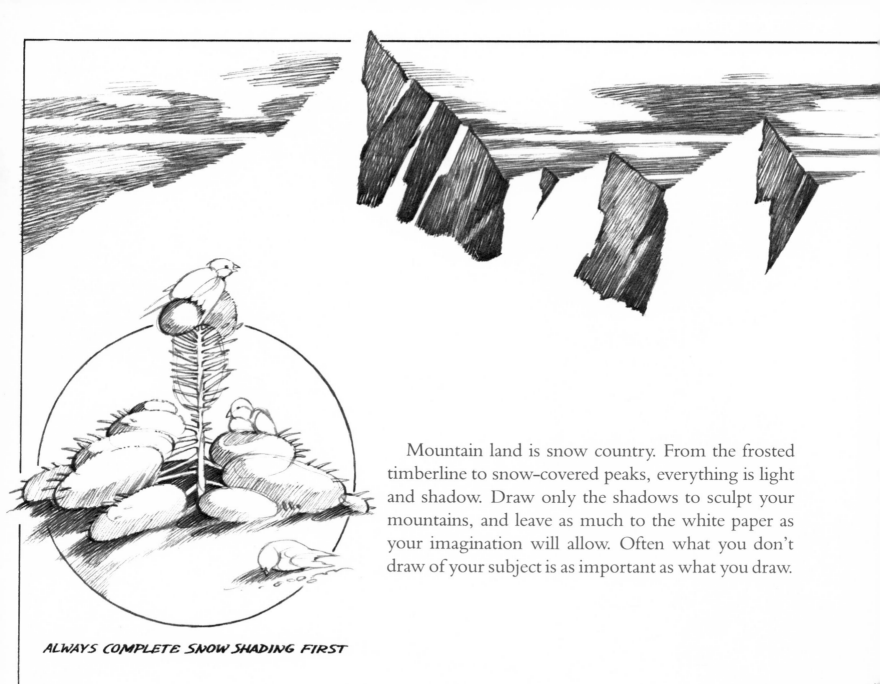

Mountain land is snow country. From the frosted timberline to snow–covered peaks, everything is light and shadow. Draw only the shadows to sculpt your mountains, and leave as much to the white paper as your imagination will allow. Often what you don't draw of your subject is as important as what you draw.

ALWAYS COMPLETE SNOW SHADING FIRST

Capture all of snow's beauty, but remember, snow is water, and water is heavy. Weight your picture with it. Show what has adjusted easily to the added weight and what is heavily laden. Suggest the landscape hidden under the snow and the parts that remain uncovered.

When you are sketching the land, picture the present with an understanding of the past. Walk the lowlands. Climb the hills. See and draw everything.

PART III
DRAWING PLANTS

I wonder about plant life. I want to know how many plants there are and all of their names. I want to find the hiding places plants have—to see their roots, feel their leaves, and smell their flowers.

Every artist finds a key to drawing plants. Some are scientific. Some are impressionistic. I like to construct plants scientifically, then add my impressions of their individual personalities.

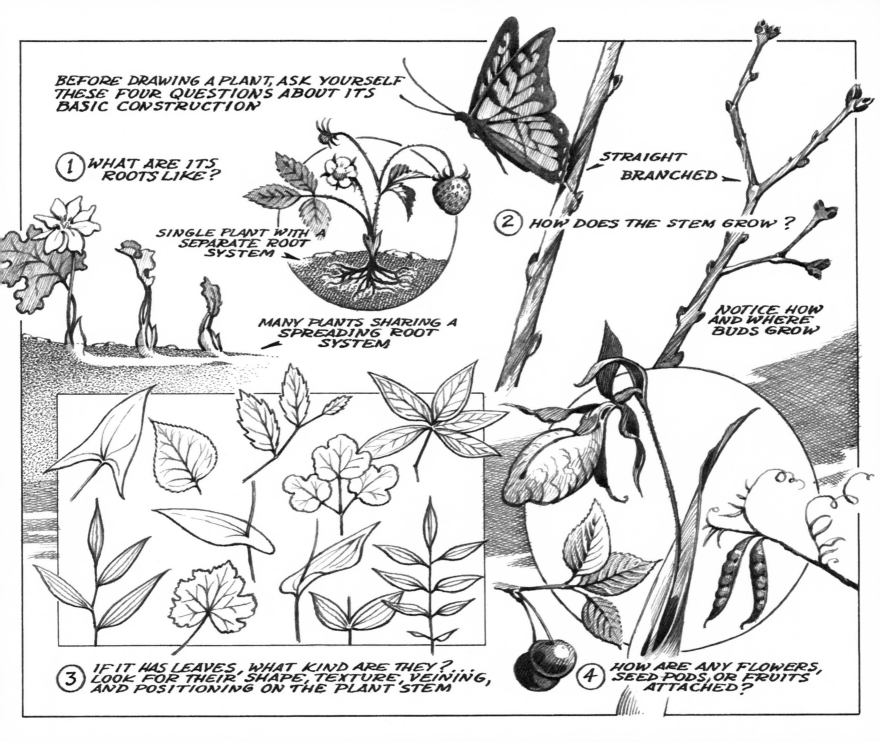

BEFORE DRAWING A PLANT, ASK YOURSELF
THESE FOUR QUESTIONS ABOUT ITS
BASIC CONSTRUCTION

① WHAT ARE ITS
ROOTS LIKE?

SINGLE PLANT WITH A
SEPARATE ROOT
SYSTEM

MANY PLANTS SHARING A
SPREADING ROOT
SYSTEM

STRAIGHT

BRANCHED

② HOW DOES THE STEM GROW?

NOTICE HOW
AND WHERE
BUDS GROW

③ IF IT HAS LEAVES, WHAT KIND ARE THEY?...
LOOK FOR THEIR SHAPE, TEXTURE, VEINING,
AND POSITIONING ON THE PLANT STEM

④ HOW ARE ANY FLOWERS,
SEED PODS, OR FRUITS
ATTACHED?

THIS HEARTY RED-CAPPED
LICHEN IS NICKNAMED
"BRITISH SOLDIERS"

TOUGH LITTLE HEATH PLANTS
TRAIL ALONG ON ROCKY SOIL

FLOWERING MOSS CREEPS UP ALPINE SLOPES

In arctic lands, plants grow on sparse soil and rocky terrain. Lichens hug the ground like entrenched platoons of colorfully capped soldiers under enemy fire. In the arctic, the enemies are bitter winds and cold.

When you draw any ground-hugging plants, give them the stouthearted look they deserve. Show where they advance on the landscape and where they retreat. It will give your pictures a sense of being where such hardy plants live, in all seasons, all weather.

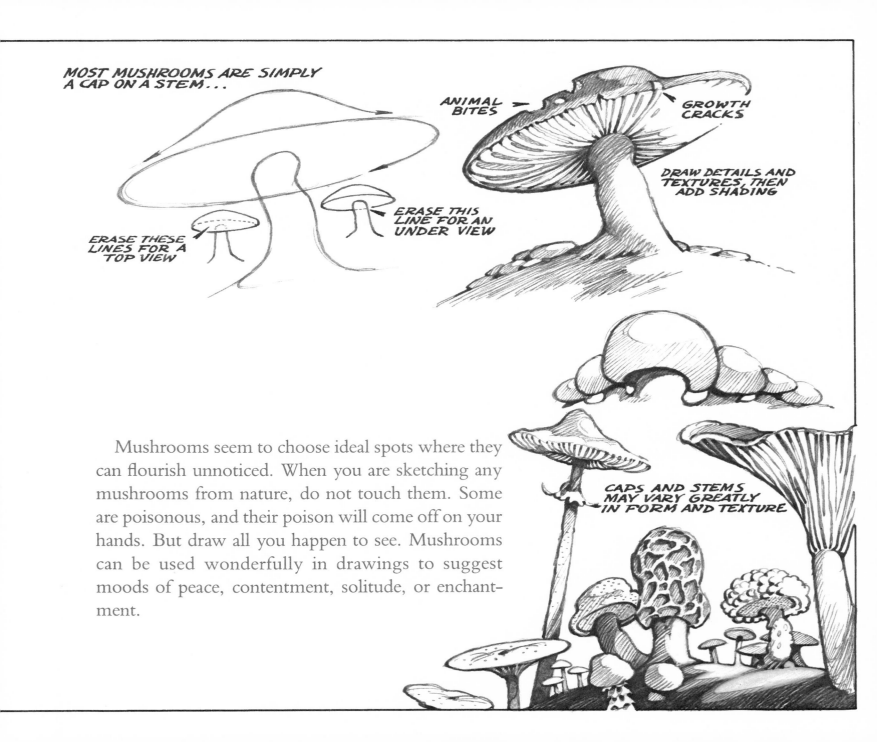

MOST MUSHROOMS ARE SIMPLY
A CAP ON A STEM...

ANIMAL
BITES

GROWTH
CRACKS

DRAW DETAILS AND
TEXTURES, THEN
ADD SHADING

ERASE THIS
LINE FOR AN
UNDER VIEW

ERASE THESE
LINES FOR A
TOP VIEW

CAPS AND STEMS
MAY VARY GREATLY
IN FORM AND TEXTURE

Mushrooms seem to choose ideal spots where they can flourish unnoticed. When you are sketching any mushrooms from nature, do not touch them. Some are poisonous, and their poison will come off on your hands. But draw all you happen to see. Mushrooms can be used wonderfully in drawings to suggest moods of peace, contentment, solitude, or enchantment.

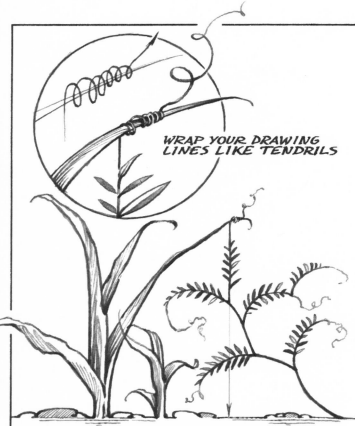

WRAP YOUR DRAWING
LINES LIKE TENDRILS

Once a plant takes hold in a spot, it hangs on for dear life. A corn plant's roots not only seek moisture and nutrients, they also hold the cornstalk upright and in place. A clinging vine is rooted also, but supports itself with curling stem tendrils that grasp whatever they can reach.

Most water plants, while they appear to be floating unattached, have long stems that tie into a main root. Anchor each plant in your drawing the way it grows in nature.

HERE A STOUT CORN PLANT HELPS
SUPPORT A LIMP VETCH VINE...
THE ARROW SHOWS GRAVITY PULL
ON THE HANGING VINE

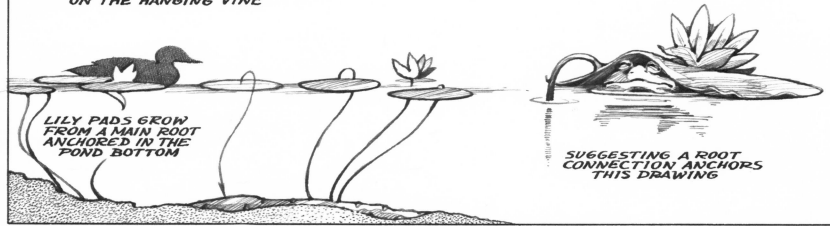

LILY PADS GROW
FROM A MAIN ROOT
ANCHORED IN THE
POND BOTTOM

SUGGESTING A ROOT
CONNECTION ANCHORS
THIS DRAWING

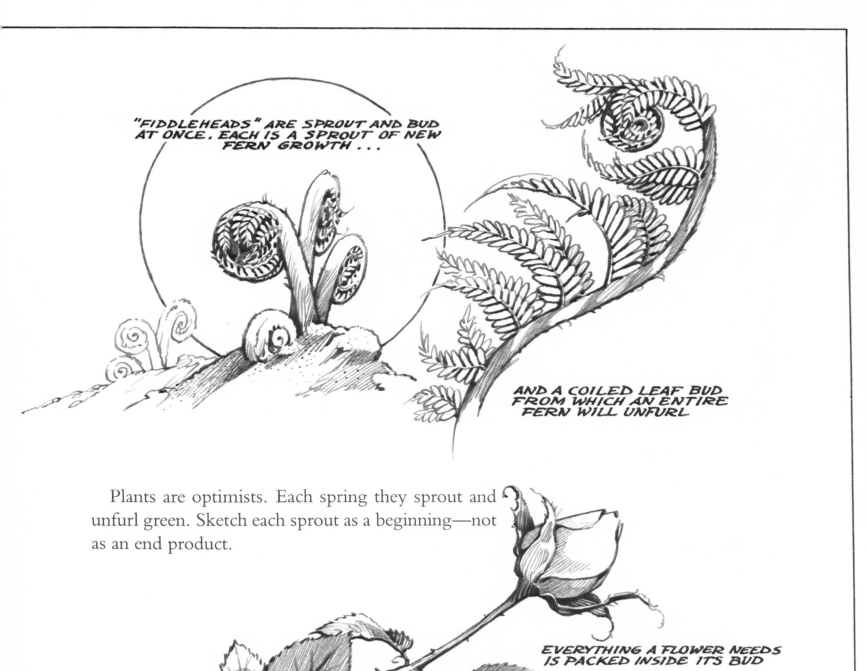

"FIDDLEHEADS" ARE SPROUT AND BUD AT ONCE. EACH IS A SPROUT OF NEW FERN GROWTH . . .

AND A COILED LEAF BUD FROM WHICH AN ENTIRE FERN WILL UNFURL

Plants are optimists. Each spring they sprout and unfurl green. Sketch each sprout as a beginning—not as an end product.

EVERYTHING A FLOWER NEEDS IS PACKED INSIDE ITS BUD

"SPATTERDOCK"
LEAF, BUD, AND BLOOM

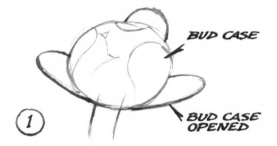

BUD CASE

BUD CASE
OPENED

①

**SKETCH STEM AND CLOSED
BUD, THEN BEGIN BLOOM BY
DRAWING BUD CASE OPENED**

Linger wherever you find a plant in bloom. Plants may be lasting, but flowers are always temporary. Look closely at the opened flowers and still unopened buds. Then imagine how the flowers bloomed from the buds.

Your drawings of flowers should bloom! Begin each at the stem, sketch in the bud, and open your flower from it.

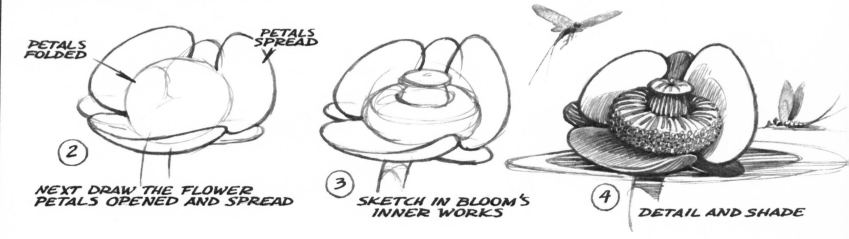

PETALS
FOLDED

PETALS
SPREAD

②

**NEXT DRAW THE FLOWER
PETALS OPENED AND SPREAD**

③ **SKETCH IN BLOOM'S
INNER WORKS**

④ **DETAIL AND SHADE**

Every tree needs its place in the sun. When crowded, trees will grow straight and tall, competing skyward for available light. Seedlings and saplings grab light where they can. Their skinny branches reach every which way, to snatch scraps of sun that filter through the older, more established trees.

Sketch young trees with upward light-searching lines.

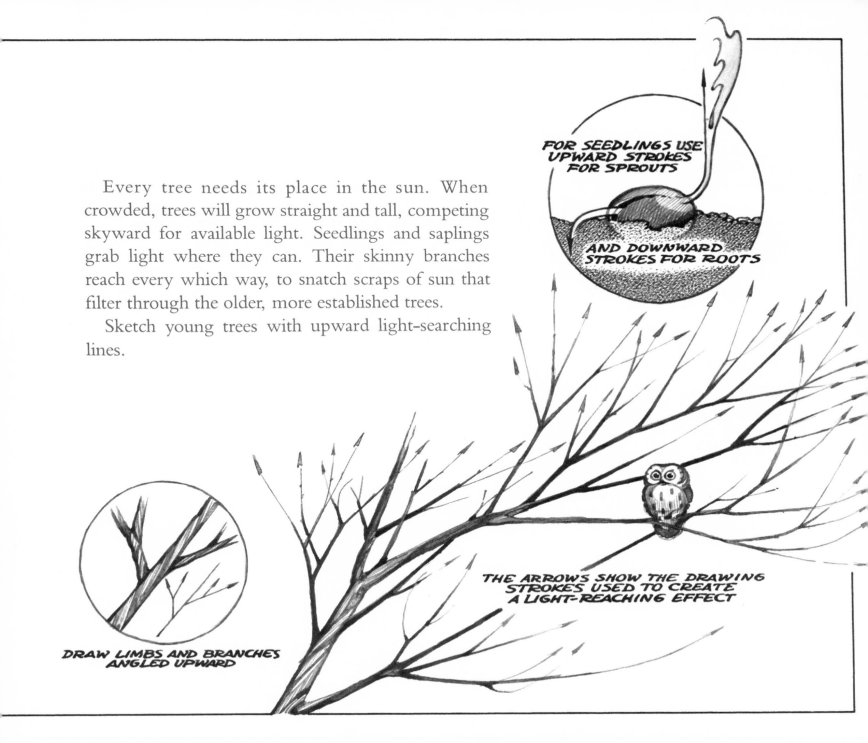

FOR SEEDLINGS USE UPWARD STROKES FOR SPROUTS

AND DOWNWARD STROKES FOR ROOTS

THE ARROWS SHOW THE DRAWING STROKES USED TO CREATE A LIGHT-REACHING EFFECT

DRAW LIMBS AND BRANCHES ANGLED UPWARD

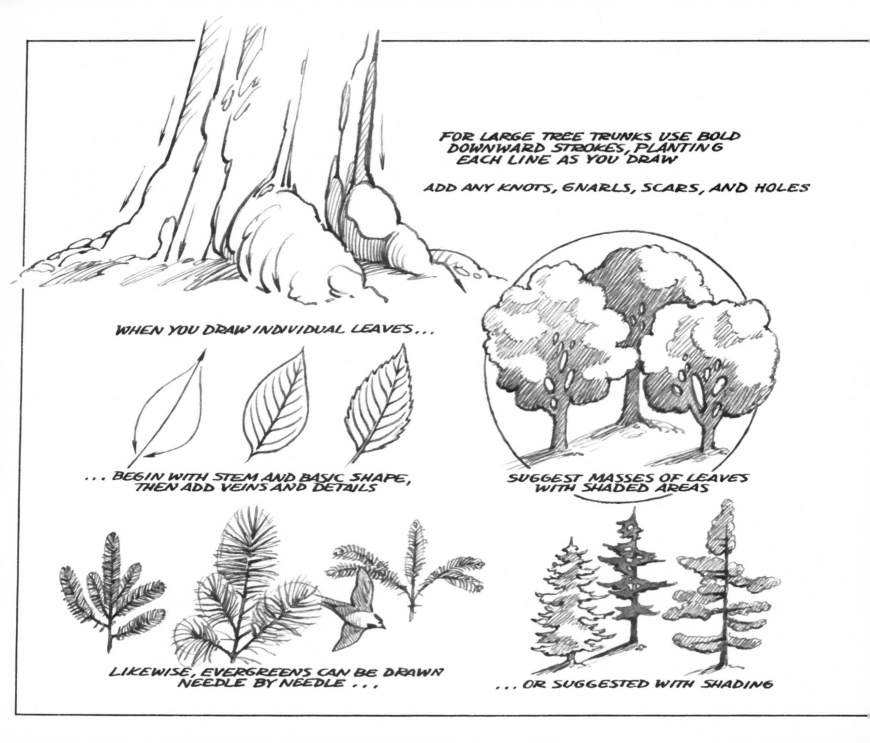

FOR LARGE TREE TRUNKS USE BOLD DOWNWARD STROKES, PLANTING EACH LINE AS YOU DRAW

ADD ANY KNOTS, GNARLS, SCARS, AND HOLES

WHEN YOU DRAW INDIVIDUAL LEAVES...

... BEGIN WITH STEM AND BASIC SHAPE, THEN ADD VEINS AND DETAILS

SUGGEST MASSES OF LEAVES WITH SHADED AREAS

LIKEWISE, EVERGREENS CAN BE DRAWN NEEDLE BY NEEDLE ...

... OR SUGGESTED WITH SHADING

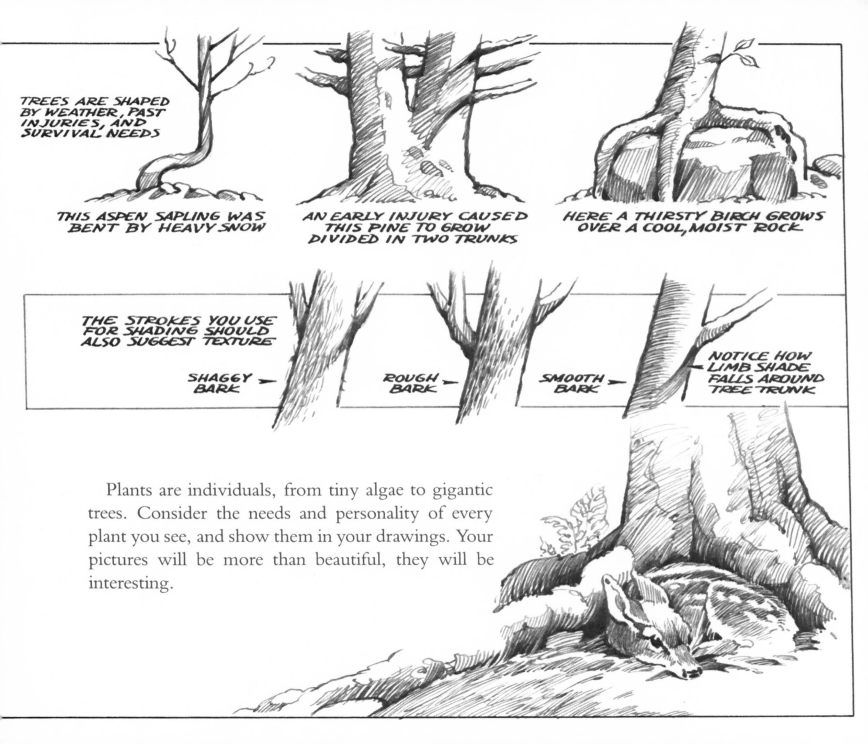

TREES ARE SHAPED BY WEATHER, PAST INJURIES, AND SURVIVAL NEEDS

THIS ASPEN SAPLING WAS BENT BY HEAVY SNOW

AN EARLY INJURY CAUSED THIS PINE TO GROW DIVIDED IN TWO TRUNKS

HERE A THIRSTY BIRCH GROWS OVER A COOL, MOIST ROCK

THE STROKES YOU USE FOR SHADING SHOULD ALSO SUGGEST TEXTURE

SHAGGY BARK →

ROUGH BARK →

SMOOTH BARK →

NOTICE HOW LIMB SHADE FALLS AROUND TREE TRUNK

Plants are individuals, from tiny algae to gigantic trees. Consider the needs and personality of every plant you see, and show them in your drawings. Your pictures will be more than beautiful, they will be interesting.

PART IV
DRAWING ANIMALS

The world is swimming, crawling, hopping, running, and flying with animals. Biology boldly classes them in two groups, vertebrates and invertebrates. Vertebrates are animals with backbones: fish, reptiles, birds, and mammals. Invertebrates are animals without backbones: worms, mollusks, insects, and crustaceans. Different animals within the two groups vary so greatly that each is a new challenge to the nature artist.

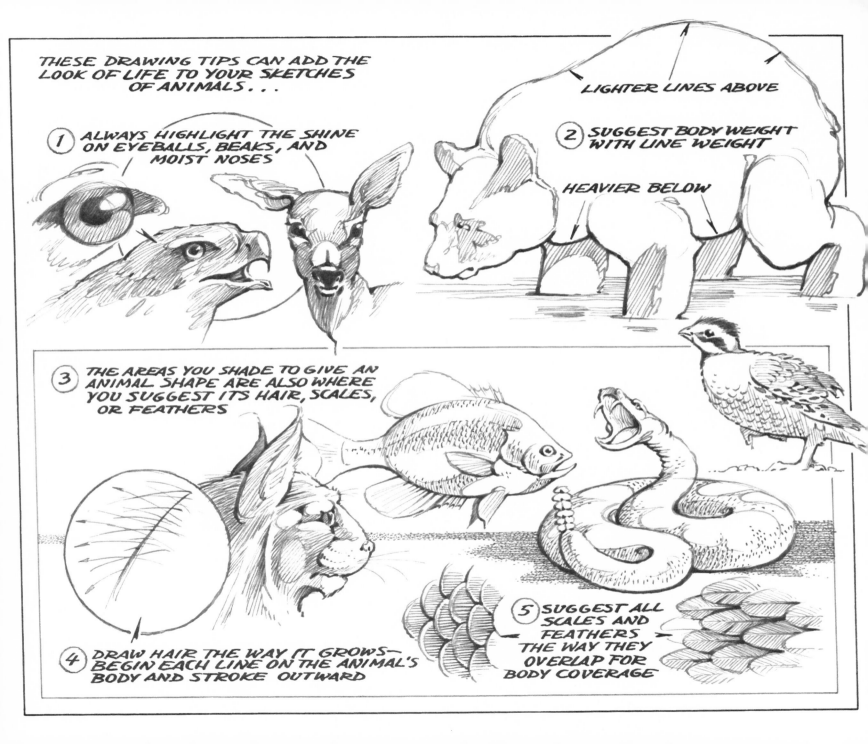

THESE DRAWING TIPS CAN ADD THE
LOOK OF LIFE TO YOUR SKETCHES
OF ANIMALS...

1 ALWAYS HIGHLIGHT THE SHINE
ON EYEBALLS, BEAKS, AND
MOIST NOSES

LIGHTER LINES ABOVE

2 SUGGEST BODY WEIGHT
WITH LINE WEIGHT

HEAVIER BELOW

3 THE AREAS YOU SHADE TO GIVE AN
ANIMAL SHAPE ARE ALSO WHERE
YOU SUGGEST ITS HAIR, SCALES,
OR FEATHERS

4 DRAW HAIR THE WAY IT GROWS—
BEGIN EACH LINE ON THE ANIMAL'S
BODY AND STROKE OUTWARD

5 SUGGEST ALL
SCALES AND
FEATHERS
THE WAY THEY
OVERLAP FOR
BODY COVERAGE

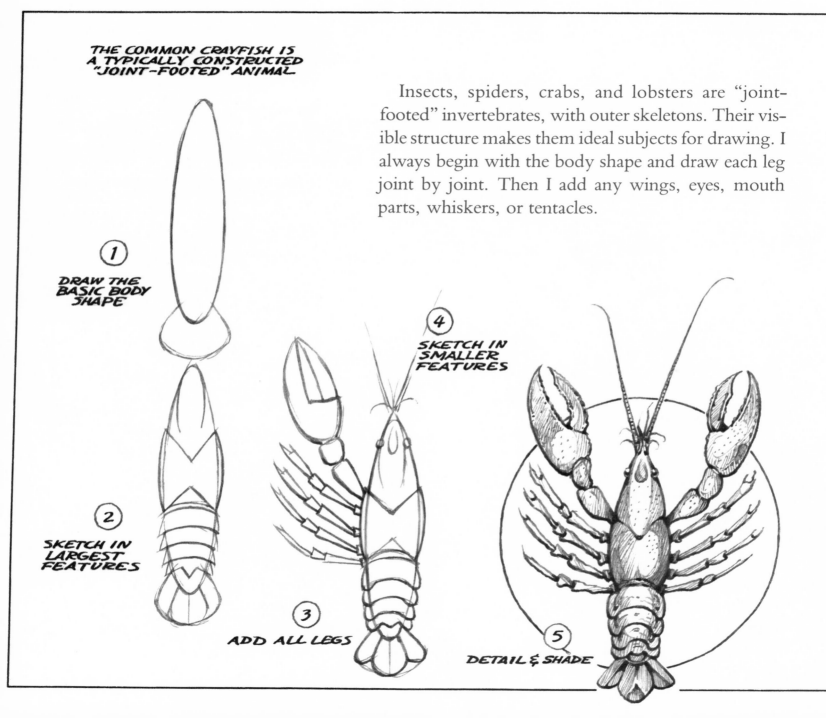

THE COMMON CRAYFISH IS A TYPICALLY CONSTRUCTED "JOINT-FOOTED" ANIMAL.

Insects, spiders, crabs, and lobsters are "joint-footed" invertebrates, with outer skeletons. Their visible structure makes them ideal subjects for drawing. I always begin with the body shape and draw each leg joint by joint. Then I add any wings, eyes, mouth parts, whiskers, or tentacles.

1 DRAW THE BASIC BODY SHAPE

2 SKETCH IN LARGEST FEATURES

3 ADD ALL LEGS

4 SKETCH IN SMALLER FEATURES

5 DETAIL & SHADE

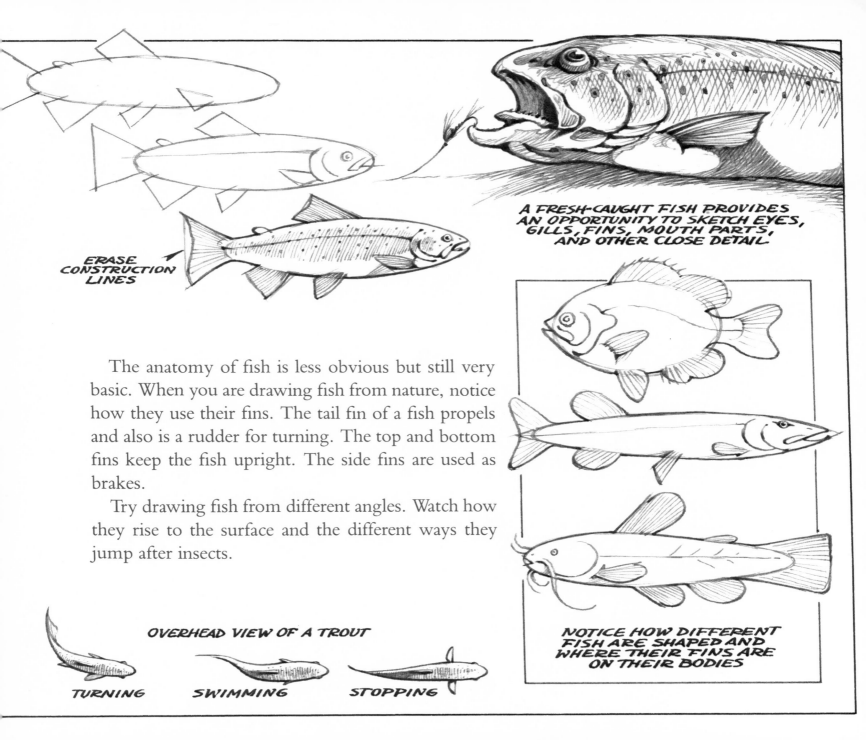

ERASE
CONSTRUCTION
LINES

A FRESH-CAUGHT FISH PROVIDES
AN OPPORTUNITY TO SKETCH EYES,
GILLS, FINS, MOUTH PARTS,
AND OTHER CLOSE DETAIL.

The anatomy of fish is less obvious but still very basic. When you are drawing fish from nature, notice how they use their fins. The tail fin of a fish propels and also is a rudder for turning. The top and bottom fins keep the fish upright. The side fins are used as brakes.

Try drawing fish from different angles. Watch how they rise to the surface and the different ways they jump after insects.

NOTICE HOW DIFFERENT
FISH ARE SHAPED AND
WHERE THEIR FINS ARE
ON THEIR BODIES

OVERHEAD VIEW OF A TROUT

TURNING   SWIMMING   STOPPING

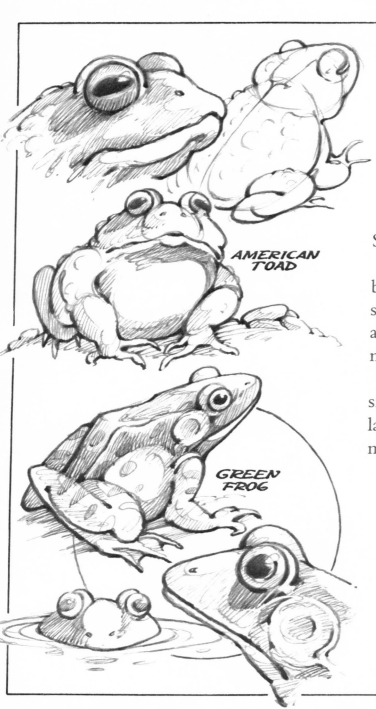

AMERICAN
TOAD

GREEN
FROG

Toads and frogs are similar but separate animals. Show the difference between them in your drawings.

Toads have rough skin, sleepy eyes, and stocky bodies. Their forelegs are powerful enough to hold struggling prey for eating. Their hind legs are short and better at "digging in" than jumping. Toads are mottled in earthy colors.

Frogs have defined and colorful markings. They are smooth-skinned, bright-eyed, and slender. Frogs have large and muscular hind legs. They are expert swimmers and fantastic jumpers.

Turtles are more commonly found and easily approached than most of their reptilian relatives. Whenever you draw a turtle or any other shelled animal, make the shell look hollow and big enough for the animal to hide inside. Also, make the animal look strong enough to carry the shell.

A turtle lifts its shell to walk and sets it down to rest. If the turtle you are drawing closes up tight in its shell, listen for the hissing sound of trapped air squeezing out. It will give you an idea of the strong muscles turtles have. If the turtle breaks into a "run," draw the way its neck stretches out as if its head is in more of a hurry than its body can go.

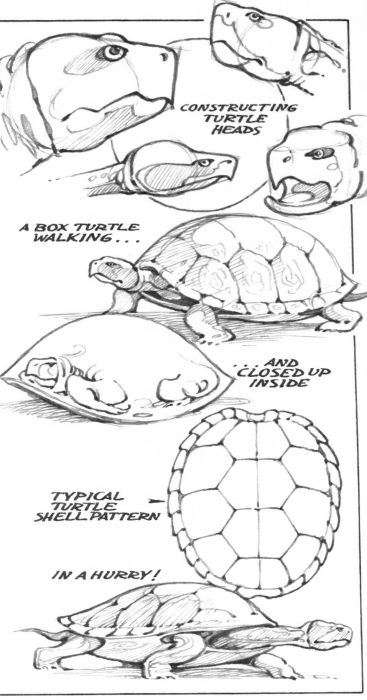

CONSTRUCTING TURTLE HEADS

A BOX TURTLE WALKING . . .

. . . AND CLOSED UP INSIDE

TYPICAL TURTLE SHELL PATTERN

IN A HURRY!

Birds are the spices in the animal stew. When you are drawing birds from nature, pay attention to beak types, bill shapes, and tail lengths. "Fold" closed wings and "spread" opened wings. Add identifying markings only after you have sketched in the overlapping feather patterns on the bird's neck, breast, sides, and back.

Draw the females as well as the colorful males. Female birds have a subtle beauty that is challenging to capture on paper.

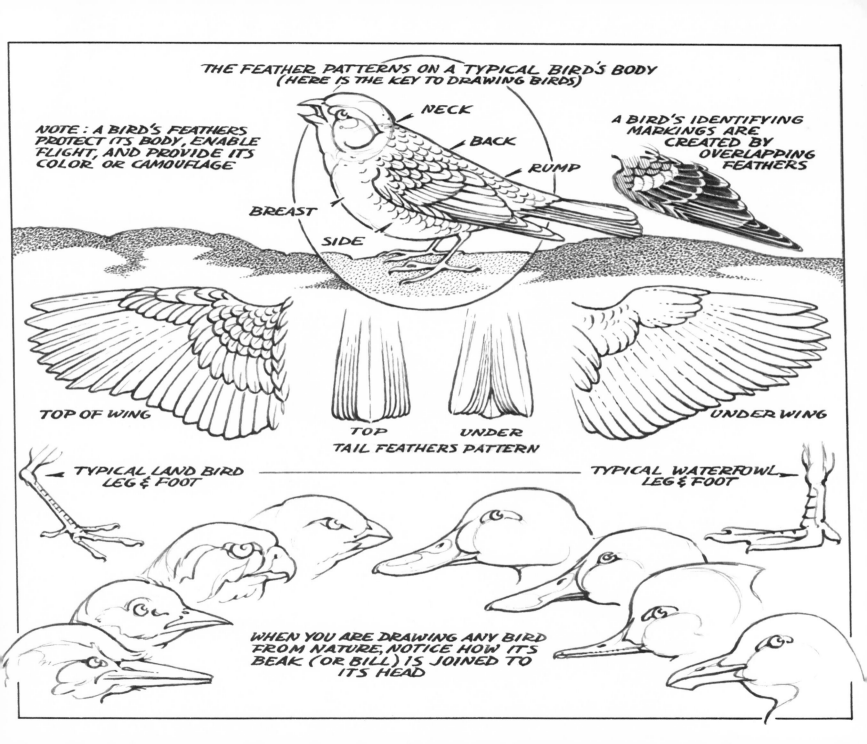

THE FEATHER PATTERNS ON A TYPICAL BIRD'S BODY
(HERE IS THE KEY TO DRAWING BIRDS)

NOTE: A BIRD'S FEATHERS PROTECT ITS BODY, ENABLE FLIGHT, AND PROVIDE ITS COLOR OR CAMOUFLAGE

NECK

BACK

RUMP

BREAST

SIDE

A BIRD'S IDENTIFYING MARKINGS ARE CREATED BY OVERLAPPING FEATHERS

TOP OF WING

TOP   UNDER
TAIL FEATHERS PATTERN

UNDER WING

TYPICAL LAND BIRD LEG & FOOT

TYPICAL WATERFOWL LEG & FOOT

WHEN YOU ARE DRAWING ANY BIRD FROM NATURE, NOTICE HOW ITS BEAK (OR BILL) IS JOINED TO ITS HEAD

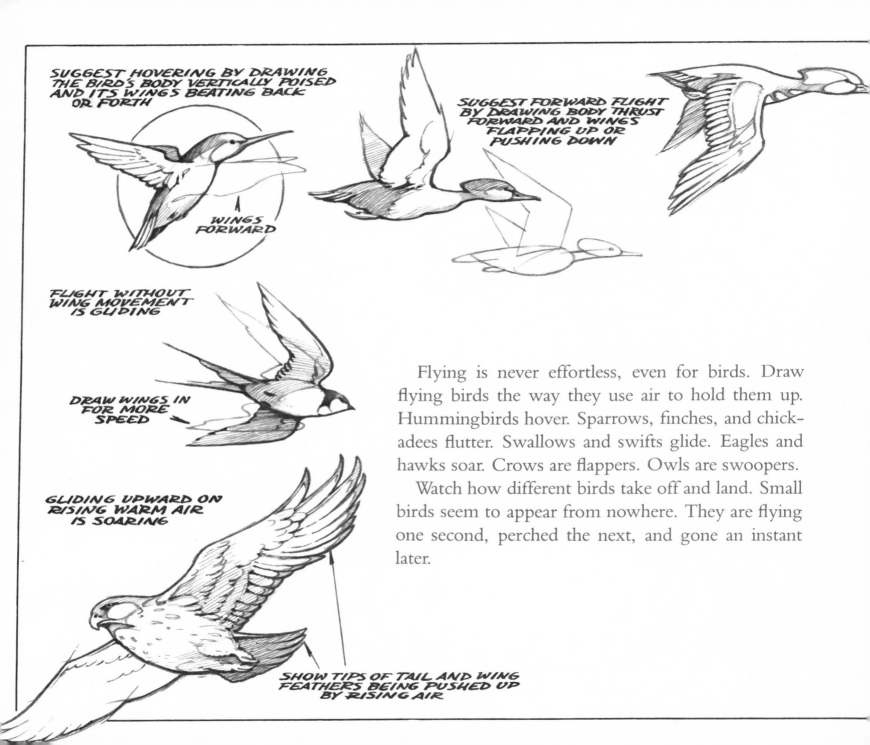

SUGGEST HOVERING BY DRAWING THE BIRD'S BODY VERTICALLY POISED AND ITS WINGS BEATING BACK OR FORTH

WINGS FORWARD

SUGGEST FORWARD FLIGHT BY DRAWING BODY THRUST FORWARD AND WINGS FLAPPING UP OR PUSHING DOWN

FLIGHT WITHOUT WING MOVEMENT IS GLIDING

DRAW WINGS IN FOR MORE SPEED

GLIDING UPWARD ON RISING WARM AIR IS SOARING

SHOW TIPS OF TAIL AND WING FEATHERS BEING PUSHED UP BY RISING AIR

Flying is never effortless, even for birds. Draw flying birds the way they use air to hold them up. Hummingbirds hover. Sparrows, finches, and chickadees flutter. Swallows and swifts glide. Eagles and hawks soar. Crows are flappers. Owls are swoopers.

Watch how different birds take off and land. Small birds seem to appear from nowhere. They are flying one second, perched the next, and gone an instant later.

Herons and other long-legged birds alight gingerly, as if they are afraid their skinny legs might shatter. Ducks and geese are heavy birds. They have to build up to a takeoff with rapid wing beats, and, when they land, they coast in, running or sliding. Make birds fly in and out of your drawings the way they would in a natural scene.

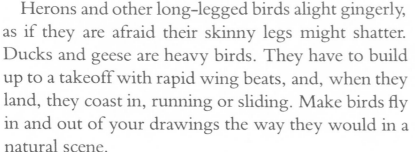

NOW YOU SEE ME...

NOW YOU DON'T!

HERON FLYING

HERON JUST BEFORE LANDING

SHORT-LEGGED BIRDS FLY WITH THEIR LEGS TUCKED UP. LONG-LEGGED BIRDS FLY WITH THEIR LEGS STRETCHED OUT BEHIND THEM. ALL BIRDS LOWER THEIR LEGS FOR LANDING

A MALLARD COMING IN FOR A LANDING

Only mammals have hair. Some have very little. Some have a lot. Furbearers have two coats of hair: a short woolly undercoat for insulation and a long shiny outercoat to shed wind and water.

An animal's coat grows in patches that overlap in different directions to provide the best protection. To make an animal look furry, draw each patch twice. First use short, light strokes for the undercoat, then usc longer, heavier strokes for the outercoat.

ADD A LIGHT UNDERCOAT →

BLEND IN A HEAVIER OUTERCOAT →

DIAGRAM OF A RED FOX IN FULL WINTER COAT SHOWING BODY STRUCTURE AND OVERLAPPING FUR PATTERN

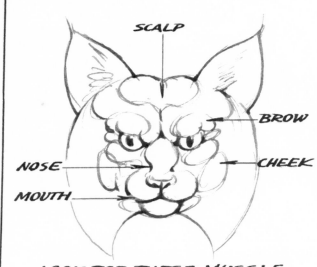

SCALP

BROW

NOSE

CHEEK

MOUTH

LOOK FOR THESE MUSCLE
AREAS WHEN DRAWING
MAMMAL FACES

Mammals have the most developed brains of all animals. Draw the look of intelligence in their expressive faces and agile bodies. All animals move by contracting certain muscles. Mammals have the widest variety of muscle and limb structures, making them the most dexterous of the animal groups.

USE THE FACIAL MUSCLES
AS A GUIDE WHILE YOU
ARE ADDING SHADING

NOTICE HOW (AND WHICH) FACE
MUSCLES MOVE TO FORM
VARIOUS EXPRESSIONS

Bats fly by flapping wings of skin that grow between their long fingers. "Flying" squirrels actually glide, on folds of skin at their sides. The primates touch, feel, and grasp what many other animals can only paw and claw. When you are drawing mammals keep in mind the diversity of form and function that sets them apart from all other living things.

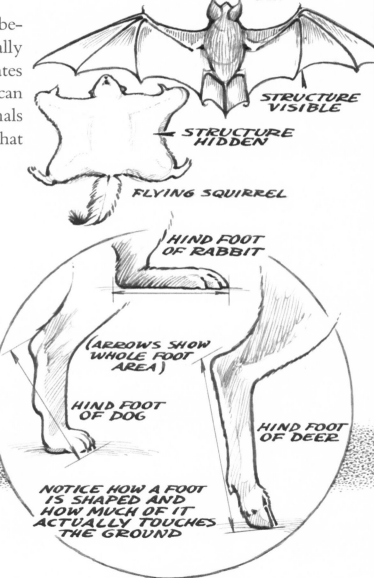

ALWAYS LOOK FOR LIMB STRUCTURE, EVEN IF IT IS HIDDEN UNDER SKIN OR HAIR

BAT

STRUCTURE VISIBLE

STRUCTURE HIDDEN

FLYING SQUIRREL

HIND FOOT OF RABBIT

(ARROWS SHOW WHOLE FOOT AREA)

HIND FOOT OF DOG

HIND FOOT OF DEER

NOTICE HOW A FOOT IS SHAPED AND HOW MUCH OF IT ACTUALLY TOUCHES THE GROUND

LOCATE YOUR PET'S LEG MUSCLES BY FEELING THROUGH ITS FUR, THEN WATCH THOSE AREAS AS IT MOVES ABOUT

Read all you can about the animals you draw. Learn what they eat and where they live. Imagine what it is like to live their lives. Try to understand the needs of predators, as well as the fears of prey.

Find out what animals and plants live near you. Whenever you can, go outdoors to draw from nature, and bring it all back home in your sketchbook.